American School of Needlework®
excellence in instruction

ANGELS

Iron-On Transfer Designs for Painting & Embroidery
by Kooler Design Studio

ANGEL

GARDENING ANGEL

WEDDING BLESSINGS
BETSY ♥ KEITH

over 250 angels

Contents

Bobbie Matela, Managing Editor
Carol Wilson Mansfield, Art Director
Meredith Montross, Editor
Graphic Solutions inc-chgo, Book Design
Designs by Linda Gillum, Barbara Baatz
    and Sandy Orton
Photographed models made by Kristie Forrest,
Lorna McRoden and Jane Meyers

**KOOLER
DESIGN
STUDIO** ©1994 by Kooler Design Studio, Inc.
Published by American School of Needlework,Inc.;
ASN Publishing, 1455 Linda Vista Drive,
San Marcos, CA 92069
ISBN: 0-88195-649-X   4 5 6 7 8 9

Make gifts that are out of this world! Create angels that reflect special interests! Decorate throughout the year with angels for holidays!

This book of **ANGELS Iron-on Transfer Designs** includes an amazing collection of over 250 angels. Now you don't have to be an artist to be creative. Simply iron the design onto fabric or wood and fill it in — painting the design is like coloring in a coloring book!

We've shown projects painted on fabric and wood, and hand embroidered on fabric. But if you have a favorite craft of your own, like machine embroidery, wood burning or punch embroidery, many of these angels will provide line art that you can use. The technique and color choices are up to you.

If you have fun with these transfers, you'll want to look for our other big books of transfers: **1,001 Transfers** (ASN 2001), **2,002 Transfers** (ASN 2002), **Alphabet Iron-on Transfers** (ASN 2003) and **Holiday Transfers** (ASN 8831). You'll find them where this book was purchased or write to the publisher.

Note: These are permanent iron-ons that will usually transfer three times. The lines will not wash out. When painting or embroidering, cover all transfer lines. Excess humidity may cause a transferred design to fade after it has been ironed onto the fabric or wood. If humidity is high, do not transfer the designs until you are ready to use them.

Using Iron-On Transfers

Protect the ironing board surface with a piece of clean fabric or heavy brown wrapping paper. Fabrics should be washed and pressed; wood should be unfinished and smooth. Before transferring, make a test run using a test pattern transfer (found on many of the transfer pages) on a separate piece of material, the same or similar to what you will be using when transferring. The results should be clear, but do not have to be dark. If you are not satisfied, try again, adjusting the heat of the iron, the length of time, or the amount of pressure you put on the iron. No two irons heat the same way, so you must make this trial to ensure success. If you are not satisfied with the results, or are transferring onto a dark color on which the transfer does not show, refer to "Other Methods for Transferring."

When you are satisfied with the test pattern trial, follow these steps for transferring design.

1. Place project right side up, with transfer **ink side down**. On fabric projects, pin in place outside of design lines or tape in place with heat resistant tape (available by brand name Hot Tape™).

2. Cover design area with a paper towel or tissue paper. Preheat dry iron to between wool and cotton setting. Place the hot iron on the paper towel and hold for 10 to 15 seconds (or the length you determine with your test pattern). Lift the iron straight up and down, applying an even pressure to all parts of the design. Do not move iron back and forth. Lift the iron and replace it several times so that area under steam holes is transferred. **Hint:** To get a better impression on fabric, especially on a second or third usage of a transfer, place a piece of aluminum foil behind the design area. You may also need to increase the pressing time.

3. Carefully lift one corner of the transfer and check that design has printed. Do not completely remove transfer until you are satisfied with the transfer. It is almost impossible to realign once it has been moved. If you are not satisfied, repeat Step 2. When transferring is completed, peel off transfer(s); keep the patterns handy to refer to while painting or embroidering.

Other Methods for Transferring

If transfer ink doesn't show up on a dark fabric or you have used up the ink previously, the design can easily be transferred using a transfer pen or pencil or dressmaker's carbon, available at craft and fabric stores. Choose a light color for dark fabrics; and a dark color for light fabrics.

When using a transfer pen or pencil, turn pattern inked side up and trace original

(continued on inside back cover)

1

ANGELICA

3

Test
Pattern

5

STENCILS

13

Test
Pattern

21

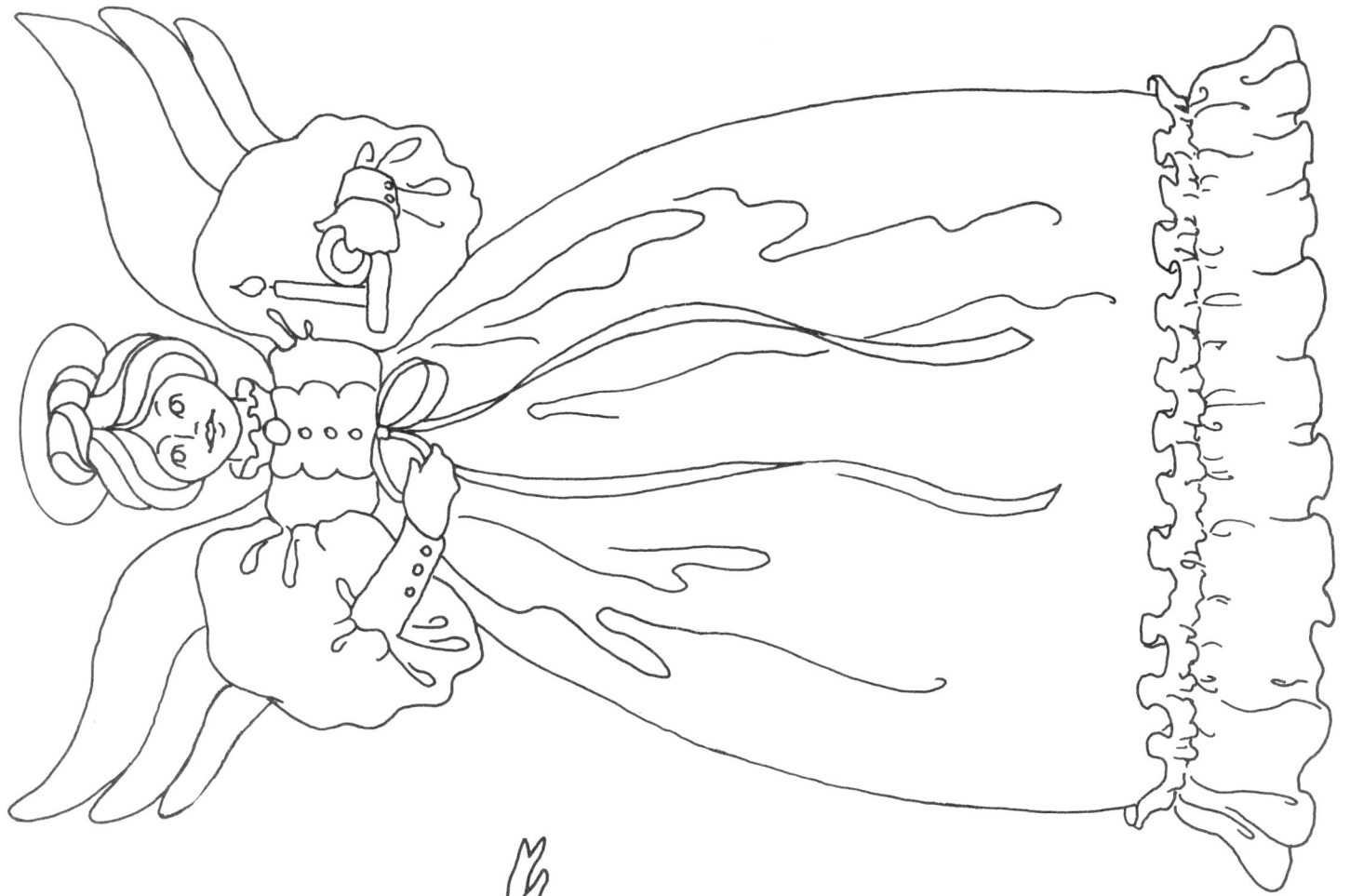

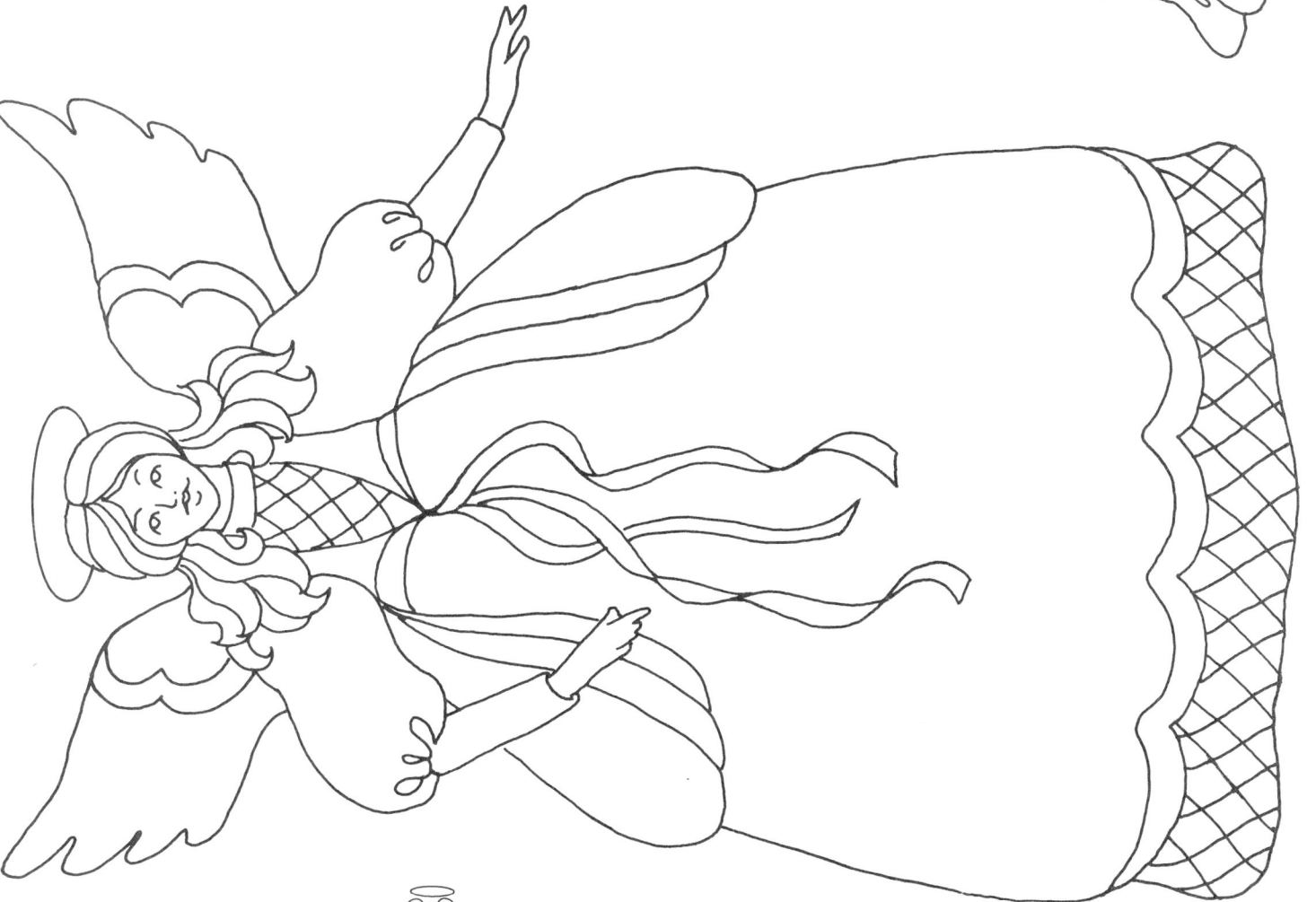

25

Test
Pattern

27

Test
Pattern

Test
Pattern

31

Test
Pattern

33

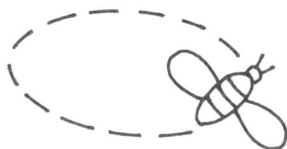

Test
Pattern

Test
Pattern

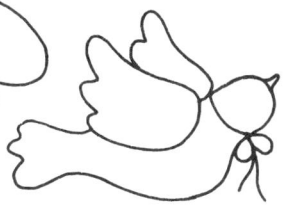

Test
Pattern

41

A B C D E F G H I J K L M N O P Q R S T

45

Test Pattern

49

Test
Pattern

Test Pattern

57

Test
Pattern

Test Pattern

61

Test
Pattern

65

67

BLESS THE USA

Test Pattern

ANGEL LITTLE DADDY'S

ANGEL LITTLE GRANDMA'S

Test
Pattern

Test
Pattern

Test Pattern

GARDENING ANGEL

rain care sun

Test Pattern

79

Test
Pattern

81

Test
Pattern

I LOVE YOU

Test
Pattern

HAPPY BIRTHDAY

BLESS THIS CHILD

BLESS THIS
♥ KITCHEN ♥

Test
Pattern

Test
Pattern

BLESSINGS
MELDING

ABCDEFGHIJKLMNOPQRSTUVWXYZ

Test
Pattern

Test
Pattern

Test
Pattern

99

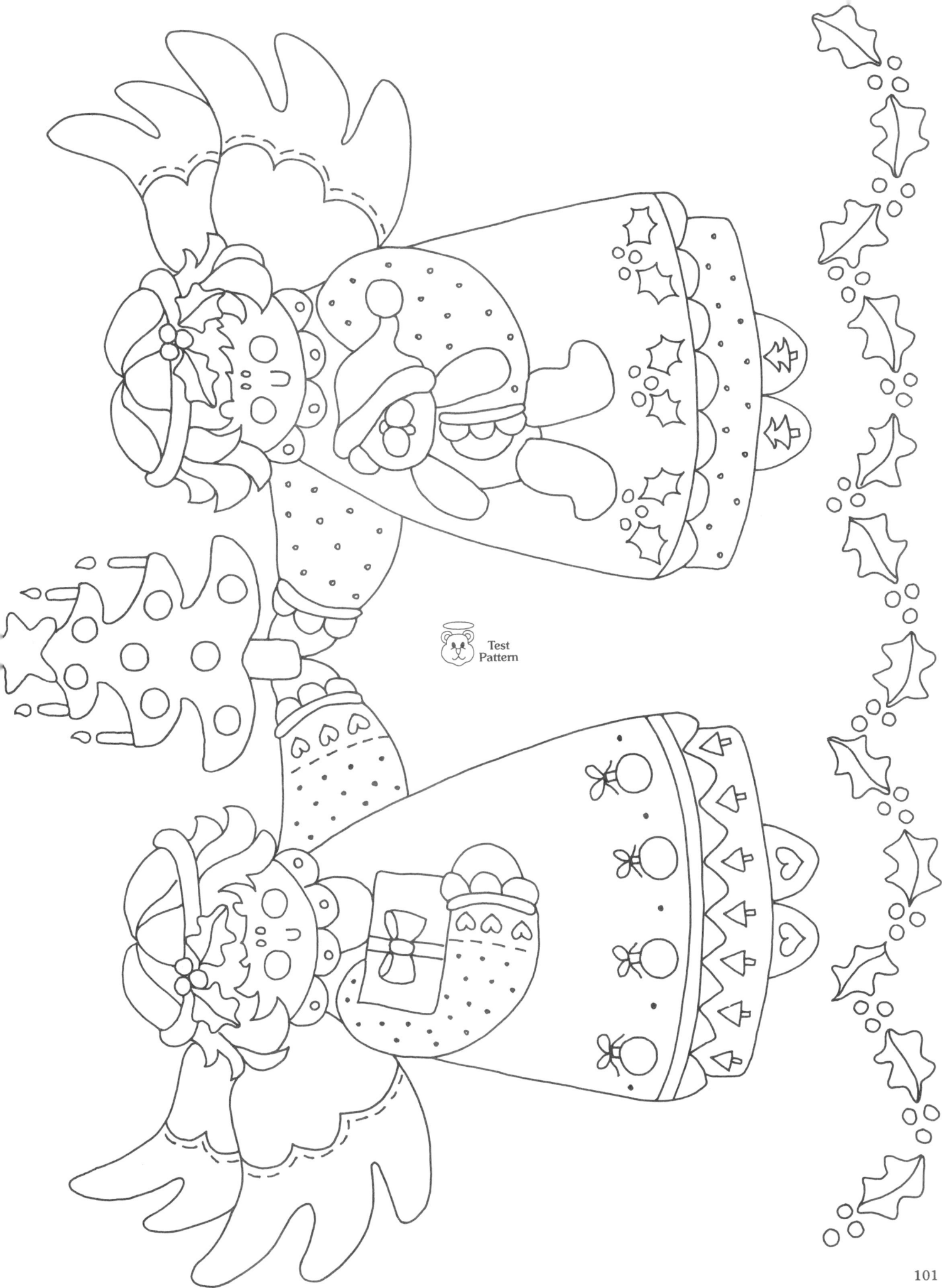

Test
Pattern

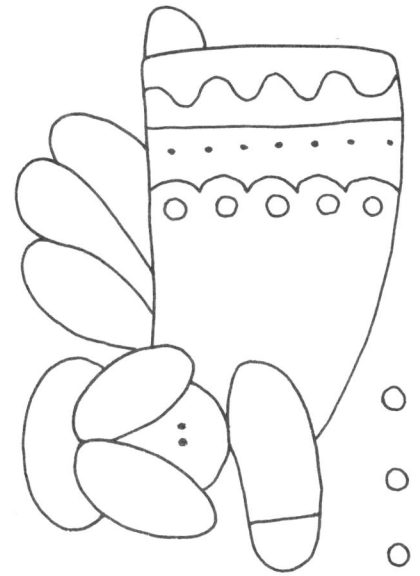

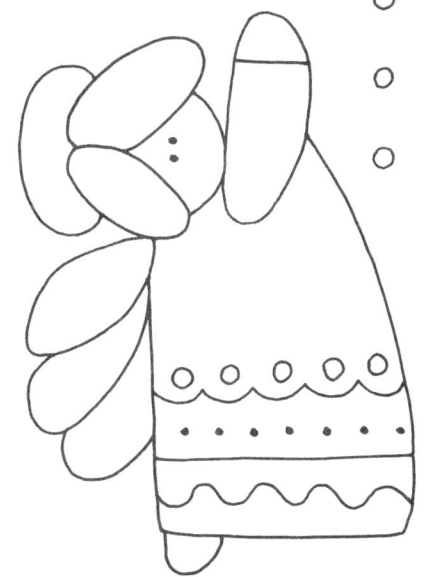

Test Pattern

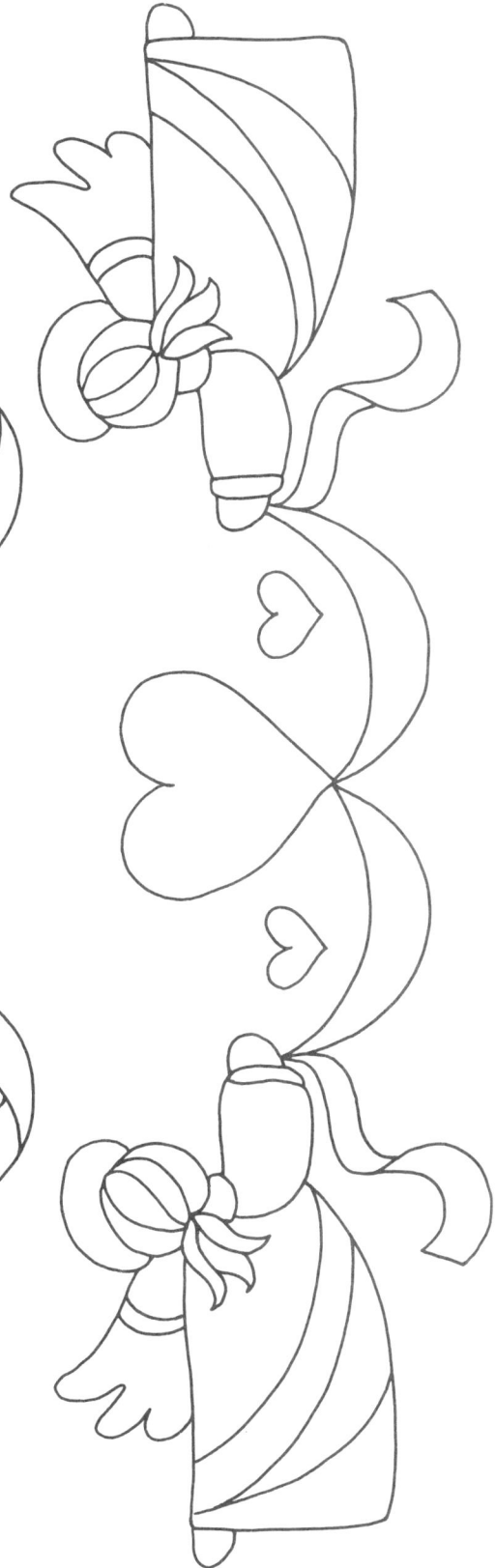

Test
Pattern

YOU LIGHT UP my LIFE

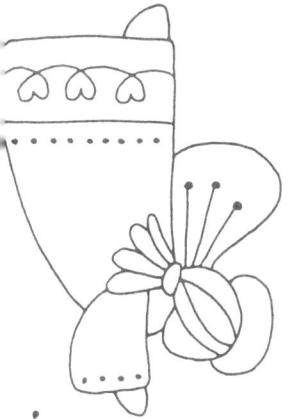

ANGELS ARE SPECIAL

I BELIEVE IN ANGELS

Test Pattern

Test Pattern

111

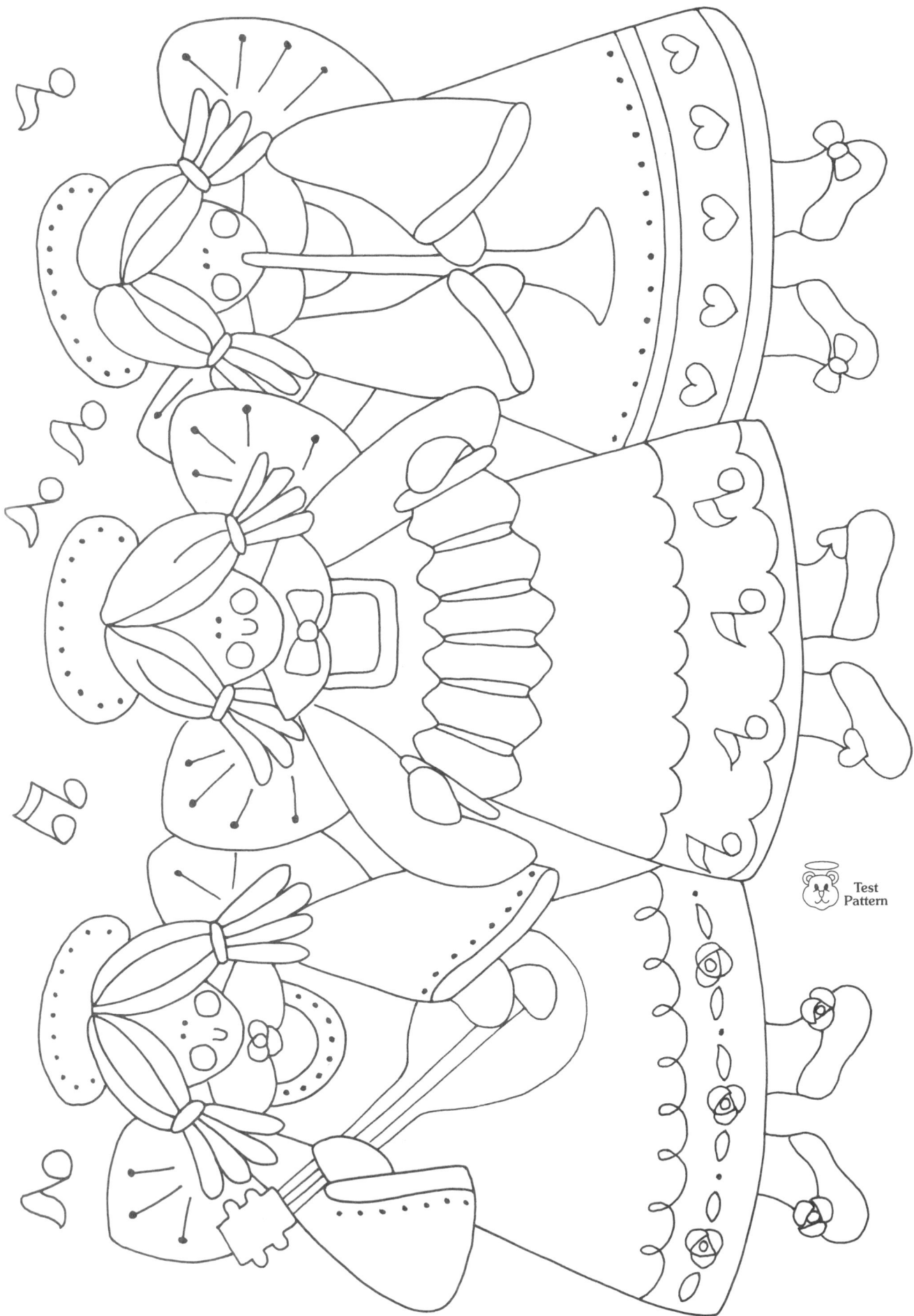

ANGELS MAKE BEAUTIFUL MUSIC

Test Pattern

113

MARCH

APRIL

Test
Pattern

117

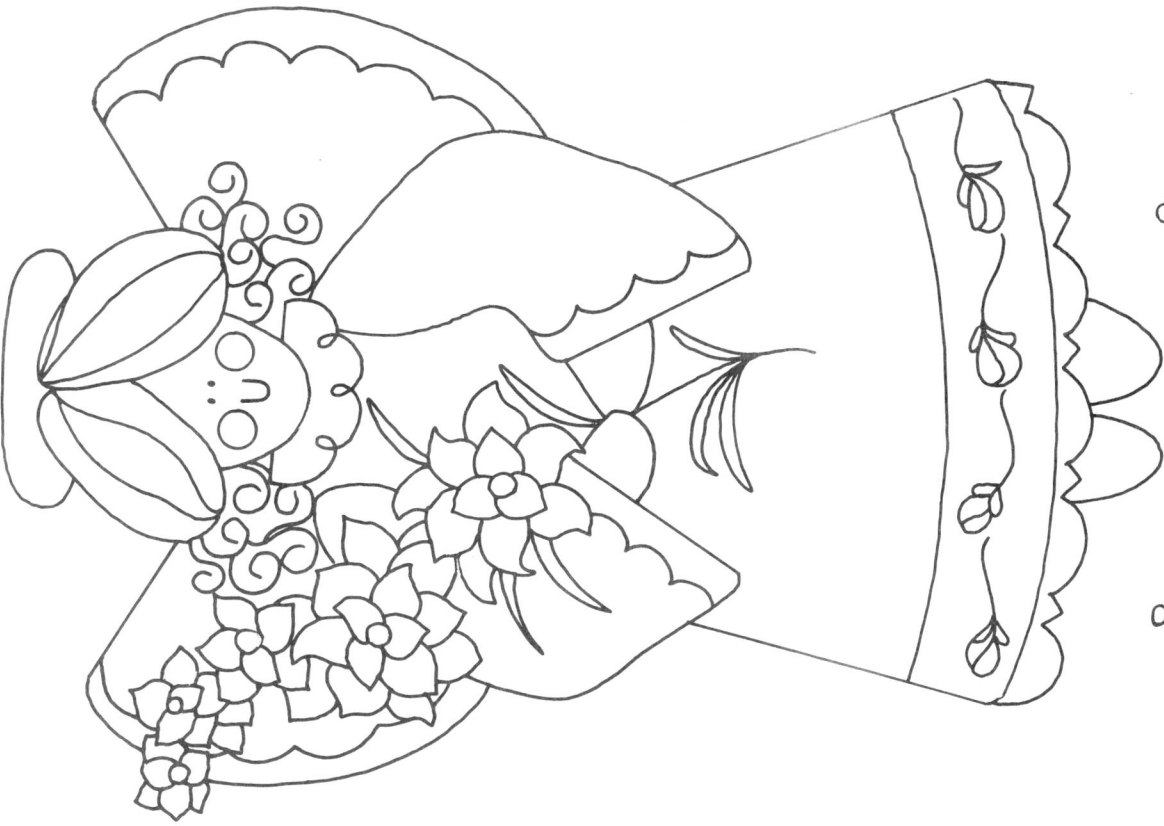

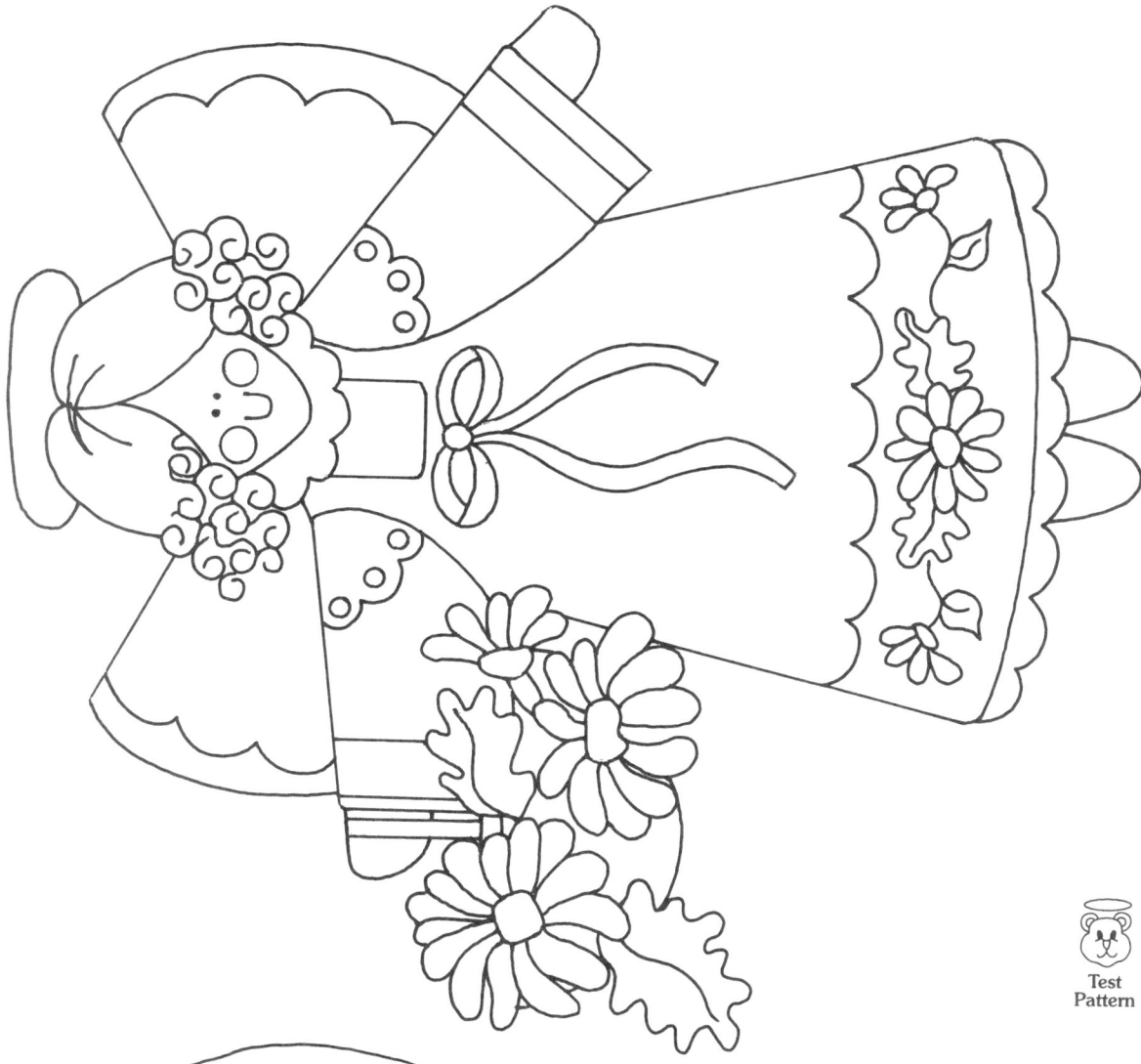

SEPTEMBER

Test
Pattern

OCTOBER

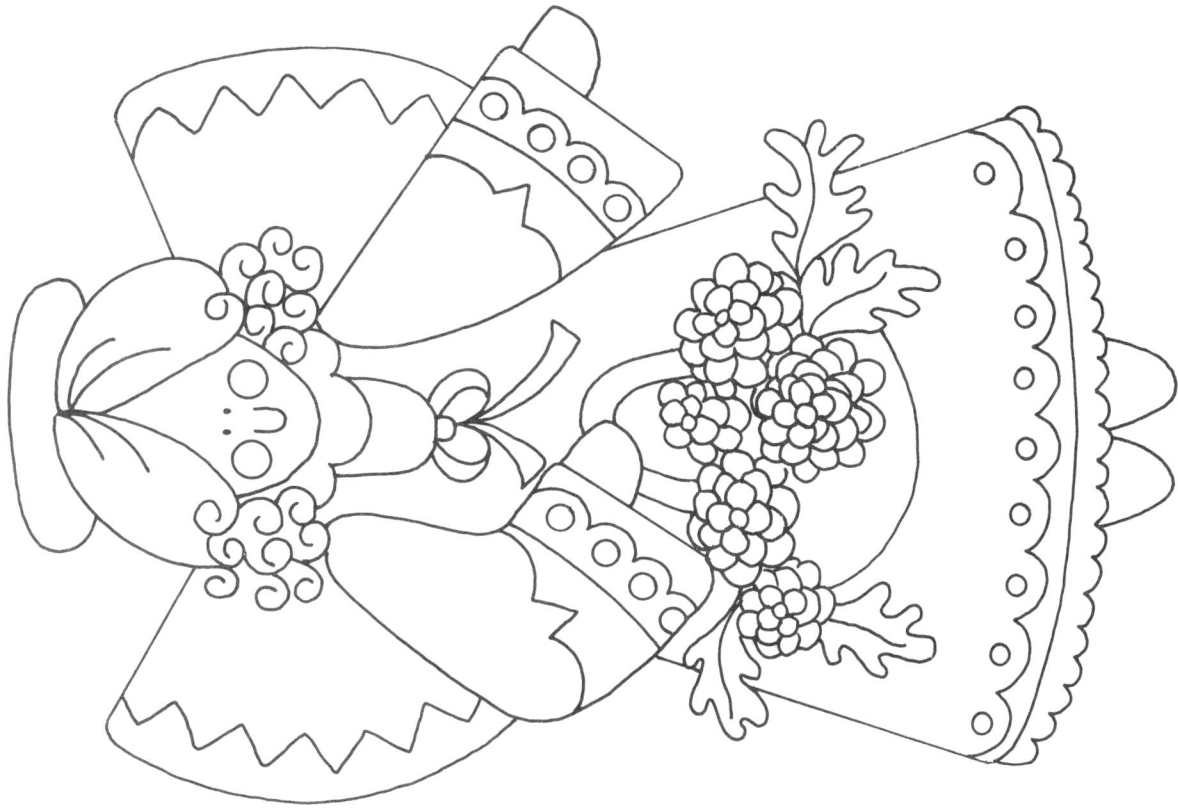

NOVEMBER

DECEMBER

Test
Pattern

GOD BLESS OUR QUILTERS

QUILTERS ANGEL

Test Pattern

Test
Pattern

129

SUNFLOWERS 4 SALE

Test Pattern

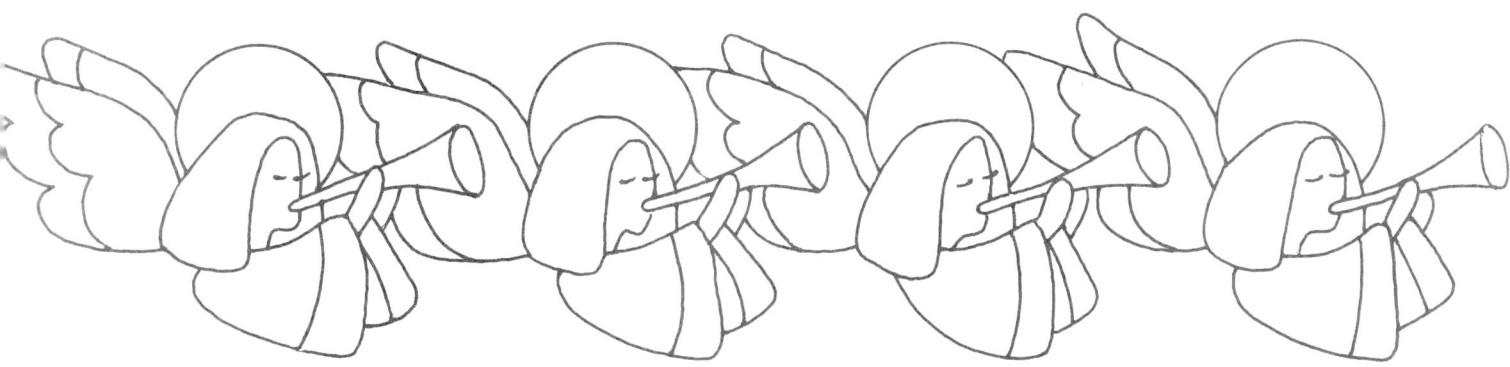

Test
Pattern

137

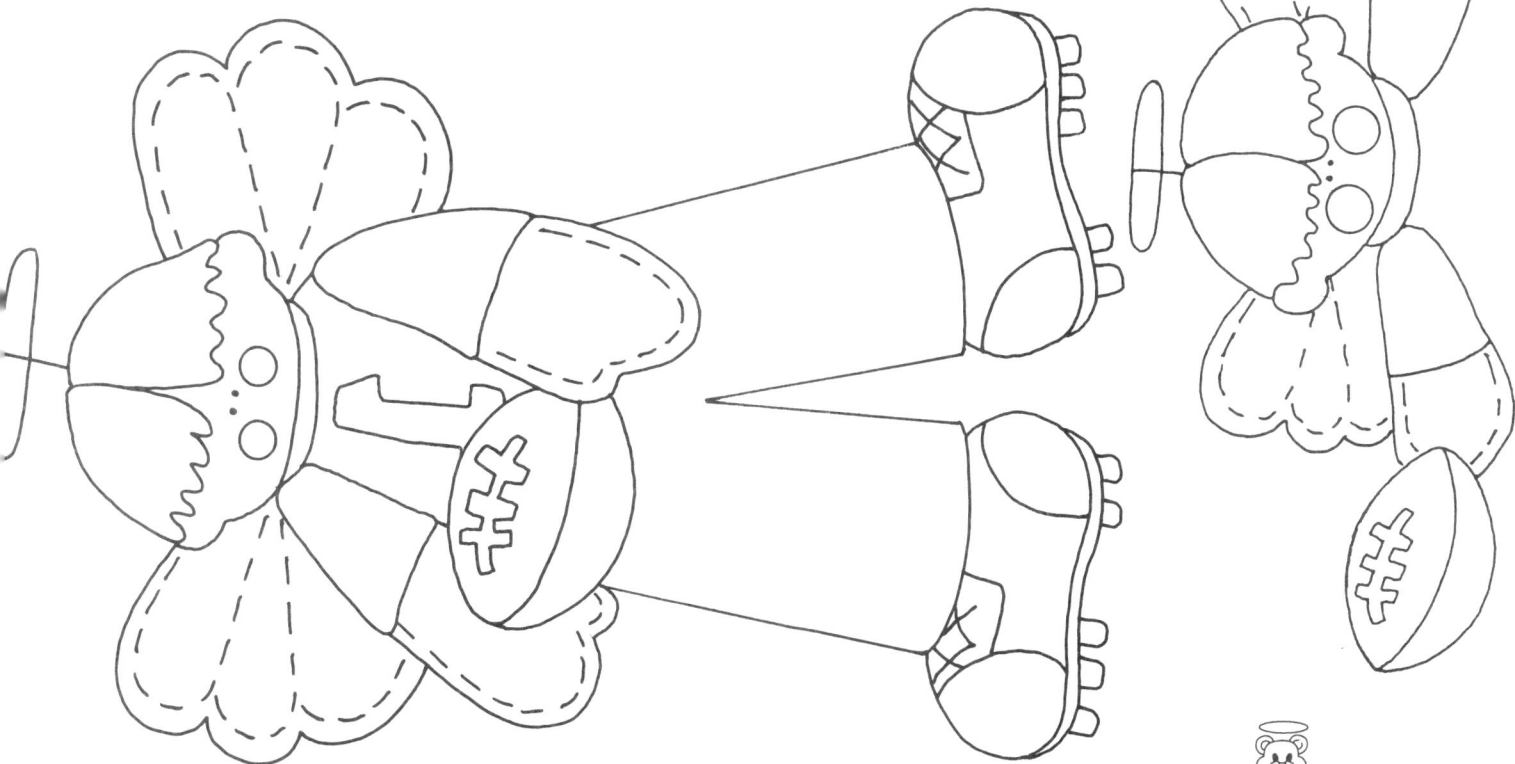

139

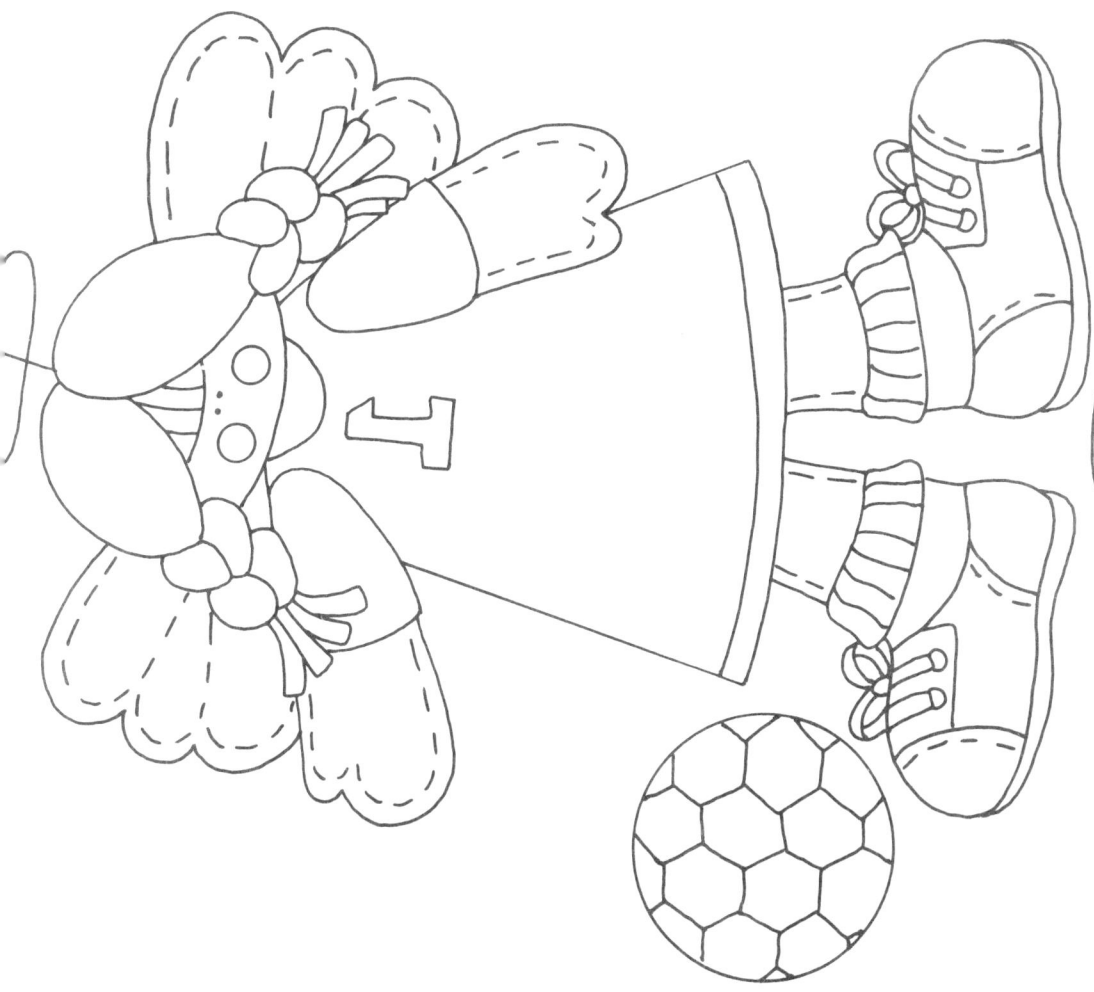

Test
Pattern

143

Test
Pattern

147

149

Test
Pattern

151

Test Pattern

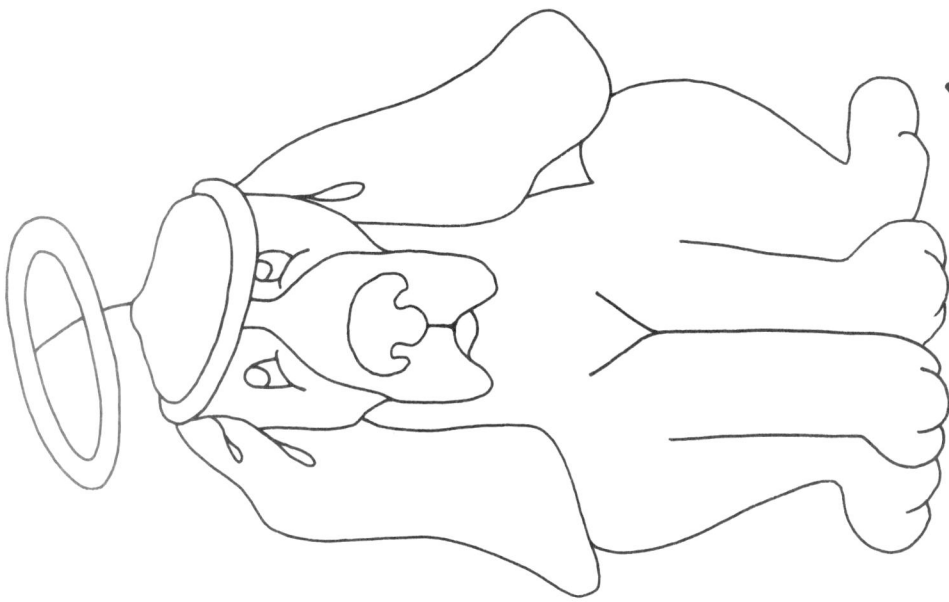

I'M A LITTLE ANGEL

Test Pattern

I'M AN ANGEL

SEWING · ANGEL

HANDMADE WITH LOVE

157

I
LOVE
U

Test
Pattern